The Climate Coup

The Climate Coup

Mark Alizart

Translated by Robin Mackay

polity

Originally published in French © Presses universitaires de France / *Humensis, Le coup d'Etat climatique*, 2020

This English edition © Polity Press, 2021

Polity Press
65 Bridge Street
Cambridge CB2 1UR, UK

Polity Press
101 Station Landing
Suite 300
Medford, MA 02155, USA

ISBN-13: 978-1-5095-4613-8
ISBN-13: 978-1-5095-4614-5 (pb)

A catalogue record for this book is available from the British Library.

Title: The climate coup / Mark Alizart ; translated by Robin Key.
Other titles: Coup d'État climatique. English
Description: Cambridge, UK ; Medford, MA : Polity Press, 2021. | Originally published in French (c) Presses universitaires de France / Humensis, Le coup d'Etat climatique, 2020. | Includes bibliographical references. | Summary: "How the rich and powerful stand to gain from the climate crisis"-- Provided by publisher.
Identifiers: LCCN 2020057907 (print) | LCCN 2020057908 (ebook) | ISBN 9781509546138 (hardback) | ISBN 9781509546145 (paperback) | ISBN 9781509546152 (epub)
Subjects: LCSH: Global warming. | Environmental policy. | Human ecology.
Classification: LCC QC981.8.G56 A34413 2021 (print) | LCC QC981.8.G56 (ebook) | DDC 304.2/5--dc23
LC record available at https://lccn.loc.gov/2020057907
LC ebook record available at https://lccn.loc.gov/2020057908

Typeset in 12.5 on 15 pt Adobe Garamond by
Servis Filmsetting Ltd, Stockport, Cheshire
Printed and bound in Great Britain by Short Run Press

For further information on Polity, visit our website: politybooks.com

Contents

Acknowledgements

This book includes material from three lectures given at the Kirchner Cultural Center of Buenos Aires on 29 June 2019 and the Brooklyn Library on 2 February 2020, which were updated after the COVID-19 outbreak in March 2020 and Joe Biden's win in November 2020.

All my thanks go to the French Cultural Services in Buenos Aires and New York, who invited me to the two venues. I also thank Laurent-Henri Vignaud for having agreed to review my text, Brune Compagnon-Janin, who encouraged me to publish it, Laurent de Sutter and Monique Labrune, who published it at the Presses Universitaires de France, Robin Mackay for translating it into English, and John Thompson for publishing it at Polity.

In its final phase, catastrophe is the intrinsic, normal mode of existence for capital.

Rosa Luxemburg (1913)

A New Front

Ecology has come a long way.

Forty years ago, only specialists and political militants were worried about global warming, loss of biodiversity, and pollution by pesticides or plastics. Only twenty years ago, people were still dismissive of organic food. Today everyone has a view on climate issues. For the first time in a US presidential election, the topic of climate change was addressed during the debates. Joe Biden has committed to a great plan to fight it and even appointed a 'climate czar'. Indeed, it is now laid bare for everyone to see with each new hurricane and wildfire that hits us that climate is changing, for the worse.

Nevertheless, environmentalists have only won

a battle, not the war. Despite the commitments made at successive Conference of the Parties (COP) summits, the concentration of CO_2 in the atmosphere is higher than ever. Despite displays of good intentions here and there, the use of pesticides continues to increase, as do deforestation, urbanization and ocean acidification. The Greens are still political minorities in political majorities. Worse still, climate denialists are still overwhelmingly powerful. The US election results were tighter than expected. The Senate is tied. Seventy million Americans are still fed fake news and propaganda on a daily basis by the Republican party and Fox News. Along with the first wave of Trumpism that hit America in 2016, politicians with heavily climate-sceptic agendas have been voted in in Brazil, in the Philippines, in Australia and in Hungary and are still very popular.

Some of the reasons for that are well known. Big corporations continue to oppose climate policies for short-term profit, if not up front then behind the scenes. Bad habits in agriculture and the food industry are tough to rein in. Pandering to populations aggrieved at the new norms and constraints called for by any politics with a vague sense of social responsibility is still fruitful. But this book argues there is more: all these years when environmentalism was gaining traction, the *rejection* of environmentalism has grown too, that is, the rejection of the very idea the world needs to be saved from climate breakdown. Some people now embrace climate breakdown; they desire it.

A huge driver of the Trump vote relied in both presidential elections on the idea that climate change is not only not real or not dangerous, but actually 'does good', to quote former Australian prime minister Tony Abbott,[1] inasmuch as it 'does bad' to others. With characteristic political flair, the former president mused, to the great satisfaction of his electoral base, about the fact that rising sea levels would wreak havoc upon his enemies, the 'coastal elites'.[2] Likewise, there is no other way to understand why Jair Bolsonaro, in Brazil, would encourage the burning down of the Amazon forest, all the while knowing perfectly well what kind of a disaster it is for the rest of the earth. Or why Australia's current prime minister, Scott Morrison, watched the bush burn from his swimming pool in Hawaii as if it were some kind of reality show to be enjoyed rather than a disaster to be averted.

This new perspective on climate change is, in effect, a huge shift in the politics needed to fight it and a new front environmentalists have to fight upon. We can no longer believe that convincing the public that climate change is real and dangerous is enough to make a difference. Neither can we imagine that the only resistances to overcome in order to fight it are technical or financial. As crazy as it seems, we now have to address the fundamental question as to even why climate change should be averted. Unless we manage to do it, the earth is – literally – *toast*.

2

Short the World

Greta Thunberg declared before an assembly of heads of state at the UN in September 2019 that inaction on ecology could only have two causes: 'ignorance' or 'evil'.[1] Unfortunately she immediately ruled out the second possibility. One can well understand why. It is always a delicate matter to impute bad intentions to someone, all the more so when it comes to something as insane as *wanting climate crisis to get worse*. But perhaps it's precisely a matter of understanding how such an intention may not be quite so insane.

There are in fact many ways in which the ongoing climate breakdown and collapse of biodiversity might benefit certain individuals and interest groups. Among the first that come to mind are speculators, short sellers and 'disaster capitalists'.

As Naomi Klein says on the subject of Hurricane Katrina in *The Shock Doctrine*, in words reminiscent of Rosa Luxemburg, the deluge that struck Louisiana in 2005 offered developers a way to make an easy profit off the funds allocated for reconstruction and presented an opportunity for the governor to 'gentrify' the state by expropriating former residents, the majority of them black and poor.[2] Similarly, every global-warming-related heatwave that hits an agricultural region spells profit for the industrialists who make the drought-resistant seeds or the brokers that own the much-needed water which farmers have to buy. It's only one step from this to positively 'wanting' heatwaves, a step now being taken cheerfully by those profiting from the privatization of water in California or Australia, and whose objective interests now happily coincide with global warming.[3] The ecological crisis is a godsend that allows 'scavenger capitalism' to extend its grip over the entire planet. In this poker game, the last man standing at the world table cleans up, leaving the other players with nothing. Indeed, the effects of climate breakdown will not be evenly felt. What's coming is not a global collapse, but a multitude of disasters large and small, spread over time and unevenly distributed across the surface of the planet. In other words, what is coming is chaos – and with it, opportunities for profit for those hovering over it. That is, essentially, white men living in temperate climates and their cronies, the other oligarchs and gerontocrats of the world living in air-conditioned jets.

Environmentalists often say that the ecological crisis proves capitalism is unfit to rule the world, and that the leaders and lobbyists denying it are pushing our societies over a cliff, in effect committing global suicide. But nothing could be further from the truth. Capitalism is not suicidal, never has been. From a capitalist perspective, the ecological crisis only demonstrates that capitalism doesn't work for 6 billion people, meaning that it would with 1 or 2 billion people less on the earth. By the time a third of humanity had perished from hunger, thirst, heat, drowning or bullets, pressure on the ecosystem would have dropped so substantially that we could go back to business as usual! Hollywood has made no mystery of the fact that this is how many in developed countries already envisage the future. In the penultimate film in the *Avengers* franchise, *Infinity Wars*, a sort of reincarnation of Malthus named Thanos decides that the only way to save the planet from collapse is to eliminate one half of all humans on the planet. And against all odds, he succeeds!

Capitalism is not made up of a homogeneous set of interests either. Needless to say, most corporations are interested in peace, and many are heavily invested in green technologies. It is obvious that the vast majority of businesses will be direly affected by climate change, even in Western countries. But in the same way that COVID-19 heavily affected small independent shops while spelling increased profits for Amazon, the ecological crisis will see money move from one set of owners to another. Capitalism is not (only) the business of 'always more'. 'Trees don't grow to the sky' was a banker's proverb before becoming the motto of the Club of Rome. As Joseph Schumpeter said, capitalism is 'a perennial gale of creative destruction', where the destruction plays a role just as important as the creation. Not only does it make it possible to take advantage of the upturn that will follow the fall, but it allows a purging of the system. For capitalism is essentially a production of fictitious wealth via indebtedness. In the growth phase, the capitalist 'takes risks', which justifies their drawing dividends. But there comes a moment when the risk goes beyond what the investor can take on, because debt grows geometrically whereas the dividend grows arithmetically. There must come a moment of destruction which, in reality, is the moment of the transfer of risk. In a crash or a war, the capitalist passes off risk on to the minority shareholder or the taxpayer. Profits are privatized but losses are nationalized, as the saying goes. This is the very moment we are living through today. Debt has reached horrendous proportions. Rates of return are capped. The question now is who is going to foot the bill, or more exactly how we are going to get rid of this massive bad debt, through what kind of disaster. Ecological crisis fits the bill perfectly.

So, basically, a morally agnostic capitalist is faced with a very rational cost/benefit alternative: on the one hand, he can choose to fight global warming, which means finding substitutes for all the petroleum derivatives now used in the plastic, chemical and pharmaceutical industries, at cost and without any guarantee of success, only to save a few animal species, keep sea levels stable and avoid unnecessary famines in Africa – in other words, to maintain the status quo. Or he can choose to leave his beloved 'invisible hand' to do the job of finding a new market equilibrium, and make a profit both on the way up and on the way down, by withdrawing investments from those regions at risk of climate breakdown at the most opportune moment while investing, on the contrary, in seeds, water and even weapons in anticipation of the chaos to come; let the pressure build until it can no longer hold, and at that moment, *short the world*. Then, once the new equilibrium is found, he can invest anew as if nothing had happened. Is it so difficult to see which way the scales are tilting in this calculation? Is it even difficult to see how such a 'calculation', however 'evil', can be deemed more 'rational' than Greta Thunberg's ethical stance?

3

Reichstag Megafires

Sadly, rogue capitalists are not the only ones to think that they can profit from the climate breakdown. All kinds of fringe radicals also do – and some of them have risen to the highest ranks of most of the world's superpowers.

Much as COVID-19 was embraced by the alt-right as soon as it was known to affect people of colour in a vast majority, the ecological crisis has not been unwelcomed among white supremacists, who have clearly noted that it will hit Africa, Asia and the Middle East the hardest. As Naomi Klein points out rightly again, ideologies always emerge at just the right time to justify policies – the racism that has made its uncomplicated comeback on the political scene is thus inseparable from climate scepticism.[1] The killer from Christchurch, New Zealand, left a manifesto in which he justified his action in terms of the need to relieve the country's 'overpopulation', in particular by killing immigrants because their birth rate is higher than that of Westerners (*sic*). The 'ecofascism' he advocated, in other words, was based on the idea that mass killings are the only adequate way to defend the climate.[2]

Then there is the idea that the ecological crisis could be desirable because it would create situations of social tension likely to lead to the overturning of the political regime in the West itself, which is increasingly popular among the 'Boogaloo Bois' who dream aloud that sea-level rise or famine will force millions of climate refugees to flock to the borders of rich countries, hoping that populations frightened by this prospect will demand martial law, providing the perfect pretext for crushing all forms of protest both external and internal.[3] Killing two birds with one stone, liberal lefties and other spoilsports decrying the massacres would soon be silenced, especially if the ecological crisis, as some predict, begins to affect not only the least developed zones of the planet but also the most sophisticated areas, including large cities inhabited by those citizens most opposed to authoritarianism, who will find themselves with no food autonomy, and whose complex logistical and communications systems will be put out of service by episodes of extreme heat, hurricanes or prolonged droughts.

The prospect of a full climate breakdown is sometimes even welcomed in the formerly moderate circles of the Republican party, as it has progressively become some kind of a gentlemen's death-cult club. There it resounds as the politics of nihilism Steve Bannon has embraced, both because he believes the USA can only be rebuilt on the ashes of democracy,[4] and because he thinks America is some kind of anointed nation that will survive anything sent by God to test it. This is part of the 'shining city upon a hill' conspiracy theory that has been active since the Reagan years. After all, isn't it true that America is an island protected from the flow of climate refugees from Africa and the Middle East, and already building a wall to cut itself off from its neighbours to the south? Why should it care about the rising temperatures in other countries? Maybe the predicted floods are even a repetition of the biblical Deluge, meant to show the rest of the world that America is the chosen Ark of God that will save civilization, as the country's Evangelicals like to think.

Vladimir Putin, who, in geopolitical matters, as in many more, seems largely Trump's puppet-master, has never made any secret of his fondness for global warming too. At one press conference he stated that he was not bothered by it because it would accelerate the melting of the ice that hinders navigation at Russia's northern border, and that there was nothing to be done other than to 'adapt' to it.[5] It is no coincidence that this word, 'adaptation', is borrowed from the vocabulary of social Darwinism. It has the advantage of presenting the ecological crisis as a natural phenomenon, one wave of extinction among many others that have swept the planet, just like the one that wiped out the dinosaurs. The strongest will survive as society is 'cleansed' of its weakest elements, without there being any particular reason to get upset about it. And no doubt it is just a happy coincidence, or a sign from above, that it will be easier for Russia to 'adapt' to it than others. Like the USA, Russia contains large frozen expanses and, for the moment, very few inhabited coastlines threatened by rising sea levels, along with a white population that has been panicking over its identity since the end of the Soviet Union, and which finds only comfort in the misfortune of peoples even less well off than itself. What is more, Europe has long been a nuisance along Russia's border, and there is every reason to believe that, without energy independence, it will end up footing the heavy bill for ecological crisis. So let the Siberian forests burn.

In Australia, it is again old white men who continue to grant a free pass to the coal industry. In Germany, the neo-Nazis of Alternative für Deutschland (AfD) are all committed to the cause of climate scepticism. In Britain, the institutional racism and craving for chaos that led to Brexit goes hand in hand with global warming.[6] The sister of Jacob Rees-Mogg, one of the leaders of the Conservative party, even penned an article eloquently entitled 'How to Profit from the World's Water Crisis'.[7] In Brazil, it is a cartel of rich white landowners that sets fire to the forests in order to expropriate the last indigenous people.

All these politicians like to say that the scientists who put out alarming reports on global warming are the militant wing of a conspiracy hatched by a powerful and mysterious 'green capitalism' lobby whose supposed aim is to subject the great nations to a new form of 'ecological totalitarianism'. This is to be achieved by demonizing growth and private property in order to usher in communism, but also by emasculating white heterosexual men by forcing them to eat beansprouts,[8] rendering Western civilization so debilitated by such measures that it can be handed over to the Chinese, the jihadists of ISIS or – why not – the Martians. As is often the case with paranoid delusions, we need only reverse the accusation to understand its true meaning: what they are projecting onto their supposed enemies is nothing but their own all-consuming and deadly hunger for power. It is their heads that are full of fantasies of 'global civil war', 'clash of civilizations', expansion of their *Lebensraum*; it is they who get themselves worked up with their eroticized male fraternity and who nourish an unlimited resentment against the private property *of others*. It is they who dream of a great collapse that would allow them to perpetuate the domination of the white man and Western imperialism over all the peoples of the world.

What they all have in common is the belief

that climate disruption will not only enable some to get richer, but will allow others (if not the same ones) undivided rule over whatever remains of the earth, however scorched it is. Or, more precisely, it will allow them to finish the job, given that the work of undermining democracy is already well under way in many countries – the USA, Russia, China, Turkey, Brazil, Italy, Hungary and so on – and that the only thing that prevents it from completely succeeding is precisely the disapproving gaze of a civil society that still counts for something (however little) in the polls and in public opinion, as Trump's failed coup to overturn the 2020 election has demonstrated.

Ecological crisis is in fact the weapon in a perfect crime: an efficient coup d'état in which not a shot need be fired, and whose real beneficiaries can, what's more, claim complete innocence, since everyone already knows that the culprits responsible for ecological crisis are 'liberalism' and 'progressivism'.

The Amazon megafires are really our Reichstag fires.

4

'So They Knew . . .'

In fact, the ecological crisis is so desirable in many deep and dark ways that we cannot dismiss out of hand the possibility that many people around the world have not only given up on fighting it, but have been actively pushing the climate beyond its tipping point.

It has recently been revealed that our leaders have known about global warming for over forty years.[1] Indeed, we have learned that the fossil-fuel industries commissioned their own reports on the subject during the same era – reports that were remarkably precise, predicting the current global warming figures to within a tenth of a degree. 'So, they knew' – as Alexandria Ocasio-Cortez concluded after one of these industrial giants was made to testify at a congressional hearing. Then why did they do nothing about it? Why did they even suppress that information and push against climate regulations when they happened to move between their companies and the top levels of states, like Dick Cheney in the 1980s, who was successively president of an oil company and vice-president of the USA; more recently, Rex Tillerson, who has worn more or less the same hats, and Gerhardt Schröder, who has gone from German chancellor to an important link in the Russian military-industrial complex which largely explains the grip Russian gas has on Germany today?

It is not enough to say they just protected their companies from public oversight in the same way as the tobacco industry resisted inquiries and duped consumers, as the 'Cigarette Papers' revealed.[2] Sure, 'big oil' is a huge, shady business that is heavily protected. It doesn't only put petrol in cars. It generates a huge cash flow that serves as a backbone for the world economy in the form of petrodollars, which are used to launder the dollars emitted en masse by the Federal Reserve Board to finance the American deficit, and which also finance the military-industrial complex by brokering weapon deals with the authoritarian countries' mafias in control of oil reserves, inundating political operatives all over the world with dirty money in the process. But oil companies are not just cigarette companies, only bigger. Fossil-fuel-induced climate change is not comparable to tobacco-induced cancer. It is not about the risk of making people gravely ill, it is about having the power to shape the world, to tilt geopolitical forces, to shift the balance of internal political power. It is impossible to believe that the same chief executive who was informed by experts in the 1980s that his business was heating the planet and chose to cover it up did not also ask whether he, his family and his country ought to be worried about it, and that, upon hearing that he needn't worry – at least not before the year 2100 – if he were living in Washington or Texas, but that huge swathes of populations in Africa, the Middle East, South America and so on would be affected as soon as the year 2020, he did not immediately tell himself: 'Well, this is interesting information to have in my possession. I probably should keep it to myself and think about how I can use it as a way of making some money while others are unaware of it, and use it as a means to leverage some power for my country.' There is no way he wouldn't have, because this is how business and politics are done and have been done for centuries. You want an edge, and climate change gives it to you – the biggest edge in the world.

It comes as no surprise that, since the 1980s, massive investments in disinformation campaigns have been made by the military-industrial complex in sync with conservative groups and think tanks. It was never only about shielding corporate interests; it was about pushing a political agenda. The same strategy conceived by the Mont Pelerin Society to break up anti-capitalist movements in the 1970s has been applied to sow chaos in the ranks of environmentalists: 'cooperating with realists, dialoguing with idealists to convert them into realists, isolating radicals, and swallowing up opportunists'[3] now translates into: 'cooperate' with the intellectuals by bringing them in for pompous climate summits that are just a waste of their time; 'dialogue' with the undecided to convince them of the existence of a 'debate' on global warming; 'convert' idealists by making them believe that they are to blame for what is happening to them because of their immoral way of life; 'isolate' the most belligerent by throwing

them the 'problem of capitalism' to chew on so
that they don't concretely deal with the climate
crisis, or even make useful idiots of them by hold-
ing out the promise that the collapse of industrial
civilization will free humanity from economic
alienation, while failing to point out that it will
also coincide with the end of the rule of law and
that they will be first up against the wall when
paramilitary militias, better equipped than they
are, turn up to requisition the aquaponic gardens
of their self-sufficient bunkers.[4]

Conversely, the rise of 'populism', at least of
the right-wing variety, is not only to be understood as a consequence of the 2008 financial
crisis. To a certain extent, it is also linked to the
politics of climate change driven by fossil fuel.
Indeed, disinformation campaigns cannot last
for ever. If conservatives wanted to use climate
change as a pawn to their own advantage, they
knew that eventually they would lose the support of their traditional middle-class electorate,
who have everything to lose in the process of
a climate breakdown, and that they needed to
reach out to new voters in order to replace them,
voters that would be sympathetic to the notion
of a nihilistic and/or mystical induced apocalypse

restoring America's 'greatness' and enforcing white supremacy all over the world. And this is precisely what they did. In this case, right-wing populism designates the paradoxical alliance of antagonistic interests that capital began to form with that part of the working class that had been left behind by globalization, felt despised by the coastal elites, and had nothing more to lose.

Of course, wildfires, rising sea levels and the extinction of honey bees don't bring back lost jobs, but they bring comfort in acting as a great leveller, a purveyor of social reparation, even divine justice, if only because they strip bare privileges and place everyone in the same state of need. A study conducted by three researchers in 2018 revealed that a 'need for chaos' was the main reason for voting pro-Trump. Responding to the statement 'I think society should be burned to the ground', 24 per cent of the respondents among a representative sample of the American population agreed, and 40 per cent agreed that 'We cannot fix the problems in our social institutions, we need to tear them down and start over.'[5]

A beneficial factor here for the conservatives' tactics is that the positions taken up by environmentalists are in effect aligned with those of the cosmopolitan elites, upon whom the working class can then blame the worsening of their condition. For the same praise of diversity, tolerance, mobility and intermixing present in liberal policies is found in the ecological discourse in the form of an advocacy of 'biodiversity', 'pollination' and anti-'speciesism'. It then seems clear to the working class that the Greens protect endangered species – except for theirs, the endangered species of the coal worker or the steel worker, to whom the Greens prefer beavers and bats. So why shouldn't they return the compliment by preferring fossil fuel to solar power?

Moreover, they could even be flattered that they understand nature better than environmentalists. Living far from the big urban centres, lots of rural voters have gardens, or go hunting, so much so that they feel they have nothing to learn from expat urbanites. In particular, they believe their vision of nature is entirely removed from the idealized and naive nature of the proponents of organic farming. For them, nature is war. Life is a struggle between species, so politics and Darwinian natural selection are one and the same. When they see a forest fire, they find no cause for concern, but only an opportunity to burn off dead wood. Diseases too are an occasion to cull the weaker members of society. All the more so for climate change: it will be an opportunity to sweep the planet clean, especially since the déclassé petty bourgeoisie often thinks that contemporary civilization has been rendered decadent by comfort, technology and medical progress, that it needs to toughen up, and that a good war from time to time does no harm.

There's no point in trying to explain to such people that Darwin never thought that his theory of natural selection applied to human societies (unlike his cousin, Francis Galton, the real author of this perversion of evolutionary theory).[6] They won't hear it. All the more so given that they are blind to the fact that they don't belong to the risk groups directly threatened by the plagues and cataclysms they are calling for. It was often healthy young people who wanted COVID-19 to spread as quickly as possible through society, especially those who didn't do jobs that put them in regular contact with the public. Likewise, it is white, occidental, often senior people, who therefore have no reason to be exposed to the long-term effects of climate change, who most vociferously claim that there's nothing to fear. And even that there might be a great deal of benefit to be had from it, if only non-whites are going to suffer.

And so we see that, over the last forty years, insofar as neoliberals could count on the support of this new base of voters to stay in power, they have chosen to take an increasingly expeditious and authoritarian turn, not only negating climate change, but actually calling it upon us. Not content with failing to implement the Paris Agreement (like his European colleagues), Trump crashed out of it very publicly and rolled back dozens of anti-pollution regulations. Bolsonaro, no longer satisfied with paying no attention to the protection of the Amazon rainforest, invited his citizens to set fire to it.

True, an increase of +2 °C in global temperatures by 2100, as predicted in one of the Intergovernmental Panel on Climate Change (IPCC) scenarios, may be too little too late; it leaves plenty of room for the environmentalists to gain power and reverse its course now that climate denialism is no longer effective. Indeed, according to these same scenarios, +2 °C would cause 'only' 150 million deaths and 1 billion displaced people. But 'fortunately', with every half a degree this number increases exponentially. If things go well, meaning 'badly', by 2025 or 2030 the geo-political house of cards may begin to wobble too quickly to be stopped. And since operatives are in power capable of making it happen, they will surely seize the moment to create an irreversible situation: a full and swift climate breakdown, as the last and only way to impose the rule of the minority over the majority.

5

Carbofascism

Bruno Latour has suggested that the elites have
seceded from the planet.[1] A UN report talks
about the risk of 'climate apartheid',[2] while some
activists speak of the beginnings of an 'Earthxit'.
Add to this that, alongside the Silicon Valley
billionaires preparing to move into secure air-
conditioned complexes in New Zealand while
they wait to colonize Mars, there are others who
have no intention of leaving – quite the opposite: they want to get rid of the rest of us. We
are living through an armed vigil, the last night
before an unprecedented battle: the most complete power grab and radical carving up of all the
earth's resources that has ever been attempted.[3]

If anyone were to doubt that such a thing is

happening or even could happen, they need only open up their history books to convince themselves of the contrary, because it has happened before, and in strikingly similar fashion, when fascists rose to power in Europe in the 1930s.

As Trotsky, a witness to its rise, explained, fascism appeared when capitalism realized it could only perpetuate itself by turning its back on the proletariat, whose demands were eroding capitalism's margins.[4] When that moment came the haute bourgeoisie shifted alliances and made a pact with what Karl Marx called the 'déclassé petty bourgeoisie'. What 'populism' really designates is this metamorphosis of capitalism into fascism happening again. While capitalism has entered into an overproduction crisis similar to that of the years 1929–33, after decades of exponential and extremely unequal growth largely based on the accumulation of debt, the haute bourgeoisie must once again liquidate its stocks, even if that means liquidating the whole world, and it can only do so by dumping those stocks on the middle class and on weaker countries outside of its borders, and, with the help of fossil fuels, ushering in the breakdown, which is why an ever more accurate way of describing it is 'carbofascism'.[5] Carbofascism is the will to enforce fascism through the rise of carbon dioxide in the atmosphere.

And unfortunately, history also repeats itself insofar as the enemies of the earth are way better armed to win this fight than its defenders, for, much in the same way as in 1933 the German left failed to bar the way to fascism and to prevent war, we are not doing any better in resisting carbofascism.

As Trotsky also remarked, the German left of the 1930s made two mistakes: the first was to think that Nazism was nothing serious, that it was only a kind of demagoguery taking advantage of the economic crisis, a 'symptom' that would disappear once capitalism was surpassed, when it was precisely the form that capitalism took in order to avoid being dismantled and to place a stranglehold on its enemies. It was in fact necessary to fight Nazism first and above all. The second was to believe that, even if Nazism were a serious enemy, it would never succeed in making it into power, because it was a minority in parliament and could therefore be held in check by the combination of republican parties.

The left seems poised to make the same mistakes today. For one, it won't acknowledge that environmental policies and, to a certain extent, any progressive policies will not be implemented by means of consensus any more. The idea of 'reaching out' to the Republicans, enshrined in the Biden administration, is a recipe for disaster bound to repeat the second mistake of the German left in the 1930s – believing that the onward march of Nazism could be halted by parliament. Climate breakdown is a national security issue and should be treated by means of the executive privilege powers of the American president.

The left has to understand it has not only an opponent but an enemy. If pointing fingers at the fossil-fuel industry or banks or lobbyists was never going to be enough, enforcing regulations in an orderly fashion isn't going to be either.[6] What has to be obtained is a total surrender of the enemies of the earth and of democracy. Thus, far from lowering our guard, the victory of the Democratic party in America calls for intensified popular mobilization.

But the radical left is not a lesser obstacle to change. In believing that climate change is only a consequence of capitalism, when climate change is precisely *a way that capitalism has found to perpetuate itself*, albeit with fewer people living on earth, it misses out the main point. Of course, capitalism must be 'surpassed'. Without a doubt, it makes sense to say that we ought to address the cause of the disaster rather than its symptoms, and all efforts in this direction are welcome. It is clear that the world to come – if we succeed in saving this one – cannot be the same as the world of yesterday. When half of humanity comes to realize that its well-being depends upon the destruction of all living things on the planet, then the economic and political model that pushed it to this desperate level must be abolished. But capitalism can't be overthrown without first addressing the ecological crisis itself, which is in reality its ultimate metamorphosis.

What is needed is a left that understands that capitalism can only be defeated on condition that its carbofascist metastasis is defeated. And that means a left that understands that it is now subordinate to ecology, and not the other way around.

6

ACT UP for the Climate

Trotsky did not stop at simply identifying the
errors of the German left. He also suggested paths
it could follow to get out of its rut. Three sub-
stantial recommendations come out of this: the
fight against fascism must be based on a united
front; it must make use of available technology;
and it must bring hope.

The 'united front' is the idea that the revo-
lutionary movement must manage to name an
enemy for itself in order to form a front line, to
materialize a battlefield, to crystallize positions
and balances of power – a front which, de facto,
will lead to a union of the left, the union of the
proletariat and the middle class, for this alone
is capable of loosening the vice formed by the

alliance of the déclassé petty bourgeoisie and the haute bourgeoisie.

The use of technology involves the idea that socialism must arm itself with a firepower comparable to that of fascism. As Lenin said, communism is 'the Soviets + electricity'.

The point about hope is that the masses who were taken in by fascist promises did so for lack of any alternative. Socialism can only recover them by putting itself in a position to promise more and better to the déclassé petty bourgeoisie.

A great deal of water has flowed under the bridge since the 1930s, and Trotsky himself does not appear in such a good light now, particularly as far as nature is concerned,[1] but a social movement closer to us demonstrated the effectiveness of these principles a few years ago, in a field of political action that is quite disparate yet surprisingly close to the ecological movement, namely health policy reform: ACT UP.

The ACT UP movement was created on the premise that the inaction of governments in the fight against AIDS was owed not to ignorance or inability, any more than is their inaction today in the struggle against ecological crisis, but to a sort of fascist impulse. At the time, there was every reason to believe that the 'gay plague', as AIDS was called, would have no effect on anyone who wasn't homosexual. And some – on the left as well as the right – even believed that it would act as a salutary corrective, since it affected an invisible population it had become customary to caricature as either morally deviant (according to right-wingers) or socially privileged (according to left-wingers). With all of this in play, ACT UP realized that it was necessary to radically change the way in which the battle against AIDS was being conducted.[2]

To begin with, the movement fought against the then-current idea that the only way to pursue an effective prevention policy was to make homosexuals and drug addicts invisible so as not to frighten heterosexuals. Far from constructing the 'united front' the fight against AIDS called for, the movement was able to see that this understating of the risk had the opposite effect: since heterosexuals were in fact less affected by the illness, they felt no urgency to mobilize the whole state apparatus against it, and thus isolated homosexuals yet more. Inversely, in affirming that the illness affected homosexuals more, ACT UP constituted a true united front by obliging heterosexuals to build solidarity with them unless they wanted to look like uncaring bastards.

ACT UP's second masterstroke was to say that technology could put an end to AIDS – Trotsky's second point. In essence, it took as a founding presupposition that a cure could be found were the scientific and financial means made available to develop it, making it possible to reverse the burden of proof and to demonstrate that all those who failed to supply science with these means were not just helpless witnesses of a natural disaster, but, once again, its willing accomplices.

Finally, the third success of the movement was that it united the world in hope – Trotsky's third recommendation. Not only the hope for a cure, but the hope for a society that would no longer discriminate on the grounds of sexual behaviours, for having the wrong face or the wrong opinions – and this allowed the ACT UP group to find allies beyond the circle of those 'at risk', and even beyond the domain of sexual politics.

A united front, technology and hope: this is also what today's political ecology needs if it expects to do anything other than count its casualties.

7

This is Not a Crisis

A new environmental movement driven by younger generations has already begun to successfully apply Trotsky's idea that, in order to build a united front, one must break with the notion that the ecological crisis affects everyone equally. Just as ACT UP did in its time, green and social justice activists are naming the real victims: the young rather than the retired, the poor rather than the rich, the inhabitants of developing countries rather than those of prosperous countries, and so on.

This polarization of the field has to be pursued to the point where the privileged are forced to find solidarity with their victims, or to publicly pay the price of their immorality. No one should be left to believe they are innocent of deaths caused by their inaction. Since the bottom line is that doing nothing to prevent the ecological crisis is tantamount to group extermination, opprobrium must be brought to bear upon those who enable the crisis. In the 1990s, as soon as ACT UP started calling politicians no longer just incompetent, but criminal, as soon as laboratory bosses were splashed with fake blood, as soon as the great word 'holocaust' was uttered – a calculated provocation by Larry Kramer – the deceitful bonhomie that had presided over the official fight against AIDS gave way to a class panic that finally had a concrete effect on medical research and on the well-being of the sick. The same strategy could well bring about faster results in the climate field.

In this respect, environmentalists can go further still by getting rid of the habit of saying that the climate is in 'crisis' (which is so ingrained that I have even given in to it here). In politics, words are fundamental, and this word, 'crisis', is a concession in itself to the carbofascist ideology, in that it suggests that the climate disaster has no author, no origin, that there is no one responsible for it, that it is a kind of unpredictable natural disaster or the result of an unfortunate chain of circumstances. Not only does it go without saying that the ecological disaster is none of these things, since it has been known of and foreseen for more than forty years, and foreseen by those who knowingly contributed to it; to say that it is a crisis is to accept the transfer of criminal responsibility from its instigators onto ourselves. It means saying that everyone on the planet is responsible for the situation. It means looking for the wrong solutions to the problem, solutions that involve self-accusation rather than focusing on the real culprits.

Typically, the victim of self-accusation will blame themselves for sorting their recycling incorrectly, when they should be questioning the very idea that waste exists and asking where plastic comes from, who profits from the recycling business, and therefore why recycling needs plastic in order to make a profit, so that it is the same companies that pollute and clean up – who pollute so they can clean up, making money twice rather than once in the process.

It was British Petroleum that promoted the use of 'carbon footprints' to make sure the burden of climate change fell squarely on the shoulders of its victims. Conversely, the only ecological concept to which carbofascists occasionally adhere is that of 'frugality', which in every detail echoes the 'abstinence' that reactionaries cynically proposed in the 1980s as the only way to oppose the spread of AIDS. From 'happy sobriety' to the suspension of the globalized trade in goods (in favour of production on 'national soil'), to the limitation of freedom of movement (not to mention the ecofascist variant which consists simply in killing or sterilizing undesirables, as mentioned above), to the control of innovation, not only is this dubious propaganda, which envisages a humanity 'purified' of its defects – the best way to ensure that the ecological crisis is never overcome, since it does not call into question the structure and quantity of production (industrial meat full of antibiotics can very well be produced on 'national soil') – but its basic intention is to intimidate environmental activists by forcing them to conform to the unsustainable standards of an ascetic life or to admit that they are unfaithful to their own principles. For example, Greta Thunberg's sincerity was questioned when she was seen *eating a banana* and, in fact, she succumbed to this intimidation by forcing herself to make a long and dangerous journey to the USA by boat rather than by plane.

When the anti-AIDS front came up against this divide-and-conquer tactic, ACT UP reminded people that homosexuals were more affected by the disease because their sexual practices placed them at more risk, not because these practices were immoral. Ecology can escape this trap set by carbofascism by saying that we ourselves are affected by climate change because we have a risky way of life involving very high-speed growth rather than because our way of life is immoral.

While overconsumption is certainly reprehensible, consumption – which must be distinguished from growth – is inevitable. All life is consumption, all life is energy combustion and, understood in this sense, all life is *guilty*, even a vegan life, let alone ten billion lives in a world where so many humans are just emerging from extreme poverty and dream of being able to eat meat every day and of owning a car. There are not two humanities opposing one another on this point, or two ecologies, 'radical ecology' and 'market ecology', one innocent and the other evil. There is only one humanity and one ecology, the aim of which must be to find a way to live a life compatible with the limits of the planet.

Just as AIDS victims did not stop making love, but learned to make love in a responsible way, by protecting and testing themselves; and just as the COVID-19 epidemic was fought in some countries without mass confinement, but by practising social distancing and mandating the wearing of masks; so the climate situation today calls for responsible consumption, not fasting and self-flagellation.

In this respect, pressure should be put on progressive leaders to vote for the integration of negative externalities into the price of the products we consume.[1] We only consume too much because we do not consume at the right price. The market does not integrate the total cost of a product, from its manufacture to its degrading. When we buy a kilo of meat with antibiotics, we do not pay the price of the zoonotic diseases promoted by antibiotic resistance (and which cost society more in other ways). When we buy a coffee in a plastic cup, we do not pay the price of poisoning the birds or fish that will be exposed to the plastic after a so-called recycling company has simply sent it in a container to the Philippines to be thrown into the sea or dumped in an open-air landfill far away from us. When we drive our cars, we do not pay the price for the warming of the atmosphere caused by carbon emissions and its chain reactions in entire ecosystems.

It could be said that governments have never integrated these negative externalities into the cost of living because they would provoke mass revolts by the poorest people, like the *gilets jaunes* uprising that followed the increase in fuel tax in France. But here once again we are being lied to. It is not about a zero-sum rise in the cost of living for those who support it. It is a matter of encouraging those who are already making efforts and penalizing those who are not doing enough – otherwise it will just end up stigmatizing the poorest among us and will fragment the united front that we need to build. That's why the yield from such a tax should be *redistributed*, as economist James Boyce suggested with his 'carbon dividend'.[2]

The 'carbon dividend' is based on the idea that releasing carbon into the atmosphere is equivalent to using a common good – the atmosphere – and that it is therefore quite appropriate that the community should benefit from dividends received from this common good. The principle of the 'carbon dividend' is therefore to make everyone pay a carbon tax in proportion to their use of this common good, and therefore for their consumption of carbon products, and to pay back the sums received in the form of a payout that is equal for everyone, like an unconditional basic income. Receiving less of this income than they paid as a tax on carbon products damaging to the atmosphere, the rich will find themselves *debtors* of the climate, encouraging them to consume less, while the most vulnerable will find themselves in credit with the climate, since the amount they receive from the state will be greater than what they have 'spent', which will also encourage them to continue to consume less. Here the forming of a united front sets in motion a virtuous circle.

8

The Green Army

There is a great deal of ACT UP in Extinction Rebellion. The most vocal of recent environmental movements, having understood that we can expect nothing from governments, has adopted a messaging based on breaking with them, and has put into practice the policy of the united front. But Extinction Rebellion is only one step in the right direction. Fundamentally, the movement remains deeply rooted in the ideology of an end to consumption and growth, which has brought them to cause near irreversible damage to their following by encouraging actions as absurd as blocking commuters from going to work. Like its model, ACT UP, it would do well to take on board Trotsky's second strategic point: making a strategic alliance with technology.

We can no longer rely solely on degrowth to save us. Had the principles of sustainable consumption been put into practice in time – that is, when the Club of Rome recommended it, or even at the Rio Congress in 1992 – it would have made for a soft landing. Not only are we beyond that point now because of the lasting effects of accumulated carbon stocks in the air, but we now know that the military-industrial complex has an interest in increasing carbon emissions rather than reducing them, so as to impose its disaster capitalism upon us. Altogether, this means that we no longer need only to reduce our carbon footprint: we need to accrue negative carbon emissions fast. We have no option at our disposal other than to *depollute faster than carbofascism can pollute* so as to win the race against the apocalypse towards which it is pushing us. In this sense, once again, we are like AIDS victims: as well as more tests and more condoms, we have a legitimate need to find a treatment and, ideally, a vaccine for the illness the earth is suffering.

Ultimately, it doesn't really matter that ACT UP activists believed that it was possible for medical research to find a cure for AIDS (or at least, that it could be found quickly – and to date, this miracle cure has not been found); the important thing is that they had to act as if that were the case. That was both the only way not to despair completely of life, and the best way to force governments to take responsibility and to act directly against the cause of the epidemic, rather than waiting for it to die out through prevention campaigns in favour of 'good sexual practices'.

Science journalist Leigh Phillips is quite right to say that if we had fought the hole in the ozone layer by asking people to stop using refrigerators, we would all be dead by now.[1] Rather, it was halted through research that discovered CFC-free gases. And today, the environmental movement should be saying that it will also be possible to solve the environmental crisis by technological means, without waiting for polluters to be so kind as to 'change their bad practices', since we know they won't do so. Our only chance of winning this new world war that has begun, and whose domination over the climate is at stake, is to build the weapons that can reverse global warming.[2]

Yes, oil companies will eventually have to be

nationalized and the banks that have financed them be dismantled, as the promoters of the Green New Deal explain. Yes, farmland has to be bought by citizens and kept away from the pesticide lobby even before a political victory can be achieved.[3] But whatever is done and whatever happens, there will be no victory without the making of massive carbon sinks.

Quite obviously, this last statement gives another good reason to break with the ecological movement as it has developed since the 1960s. Many environmentalists warn of the risks posed by any artificial action on climate. The political problems are huge ('who has the right to manipulate the climate?'). We also know that climate engineering is the solution of choice for the most polluting industries, which foresee themselves being able to continue with business as usual as if nothing had happened. And who needs enemies when geo-engineering has friends who advocate eugenics and defend fertilizers or pesticides on the pretext that 'the green revolution has provided food for so many people'? But by excluding geo-engineering from their ecological principles, the Greens not only concede that industrialists are the only ones who have the right to act on the climate (namely, to continue to heat it up), but betray a part of what they are.[4]

Ecology is a science. It was born of the computer modelling of the climate made possible by increases in computational power and advances in the understanding of thermodynamic processes. In other words, it taught us that the earth is not a deity, that it has nothing sacred or magical about it. The earth is a 'dissipative system', to use Ilya Prigogine's term, a thermodynamic system maintained in an unstable equilibrium state through a complex exchange between incoming and outgoing energy flows. It does not tell us that we have no right to act on these flows. Provided that we invent ways of acting on the climate that are themselves in line with the thermodynamic essence of Gaia, then green geo-engineering is quite possible.[5]

We all agree that it is out of the question to disperse aerosols into the atmosphere to lower the temperature of the earth. This would be like putting a wet cloth on the forehead of a person who has a temperature because they are suffering from septicaemia. It is also clear that the 'reforestation' promoted by airlines to fight global warming is a huge joke. It would take more land and more time than we have to achieve even the tiniest lowering of temperatures. But it is also indisputable that forests, oceans and farmland are natural carbon sinks that we need to learn to handle better. Biologists have invented genetically modified wild herbs that absorb a hundred times more carbon than their ordinary counterparts, and could be planted across all the neglected areas of cities. Others have invented machines to pump carbon from the air and allow it to be transformed back into fuel, thanks to algae whose metabolization of carbon is four hundred times more efficient than that of trees. If the countries participating in COP21 had committed significant funds to research like this instead of setting up their carbon trading schemes, which have succeeded only in enriching speculators and crooks without reducing emissions one iota, we might already have the beginnings of a solution before us.[6]

Once again, environmentalists need not be convinced that these weapons are the remedy that the earth needs: the essential thing is that they are at once the only way of not losing hope in the possibility of fighting the carbofascists at their own game, and the only way of getting something from our governments who are held hostage by them. As the fight against AIDS also taught us, 'If your demands are too vague and too large, you can't win.'[7] Our demands are too large. We demand the global decrease of carbon emissions, but we have no way of monitoring Chinese, Russian or Indian power plants, let alone enforcing any kind of legislation. We can't even manage it for Australian coal mines or Canadian fracking sites! Instead, we must ask each state to increase their *stock of negative emissions*, that is, their capacity for the production of carbon storage. That's directly measurable.[8] It is not based on the vague commitment of public actors to put pressure on indeterminate private actors to limit their carbon emissions in an indeterminate future, emissions whose nature is unknown to anyone else than them, since the authorities responsible for controlling them are powerless to do so or are drowned out by lobbies, as we saw with Dieselgate.[9] With this type of demand, it becomes possible to hold those governments to account for their commitments. They don't want to be accused of complicity with carbofascism? Well, they now have a way to prove that they are better than that.

We must demand that public money be massively invested, and traceably, in the building of these capacities, along with research into bioplastics, biocarbon, cultured food, renewable energy . . . The 'carbon dividend' must be enforced until further notice. Unions must show their solidarity with the young by calling for workers to join their Friday climate strikes (or rather, workers should join their children and take them seriously). We could even do with having a prime-time TV show like the French Telethon, to inform citizens once a year of the risks they run, and to give an update on progress made by the public powers to counter it.

More generally, it is essential that an 'ecological emergency' be declared to enshrine this action and, above all, that it should be defined precisely. If the notion of a state of emergency has any meaning whatsoever, it must indeed go hand in hand with the creation of a specialized military unit to oppose it – a 'Green Army', just as Trotsky created the 'Red Army' – charged with both coordinating the wartime effort needed to decarbonize our societies and anticipating possible breakdowns in supply chains. This no doubt would still displease the most traditional Greens, whose commitment to the cause goes back to the anti-militarism and pacifism of the 1960s; but the truth is that we must take the fight against the ecological crisis seriously, and tackle it with the full power of the state apparatus – otherwise it's all just hot air.[10] *Mean Greens* are needed.

9

Gaia Must Not Be Deprived of Her Hopes

Finally, Trotsky talked about hope. In Sartre's play *Nekrassov*, a capitalist who has understood the link between nihilism and capitalism keeps repeating 'the workers of Billancourt must be deprived of their hopes'. His lesson has been well learned. Above we mentioned the penultimate film in the *Avengers* franchise, *Infinity Wars*, where Thanos eliminates half of the human population after bringing together magical powers of unparalleled potential. It is significant that it did not occur to the scriptwriters that, with all the powers of the universe in his hand, he could instead just remove half the carbon atoms in the atmosphere. This tells us everything we need to know about the deadly conditioning that Hollywood tries to operate upon us. And even if the last part of the saga, *Endgame*, shows our superheroes regaining the upper hand, the ending doesn't change anything. Thanos is defeated, but the ecological crisis that motivated his action remains unresolved.

Undoubtedly, cinema, television and advertising continually dangle before us dream destinations, luxury hotels, heavenly beaches and five-star restaurants, but these promises of hedonism are not made so as to give us back hope. They are in fact the necessary complement to despair. It is a question of discouraging collective struggle in favour of withdrawal. As psychoanalysts well know, death is in no way incompatible with lust. Quite the opposite, in fact. The end of the world is the promise of enjoyment without moral judgement, at last, since no one will be left after us to judge.[1] There is a certain solidarity between nihilism and consumerism. Distilling powerlessness to change the world and promoting the sappy philosophies of personal development, self-help and *carpe diem* – such is the goal achieved through the alternation of programmes that depict the world sometimes as an artificial paradise and sometimes as an equally artificial hell, making people believe that it's a place full of murderers, psychopaths and rapists – that is, a place where no one can be counted on, and therefore no common task can be undertaken.[2]

It seems that only the social sciences are still resisting this twofold call of emptiness, perhaps because they have to struggle with the frontal assault delivered on them by pamphleteers that appear to come straight out of the 1930s. But the social sciences are also gradually losing ground to the invasion of zombie intellectuals, perhaps precisely because they didn't understand that these were zombies, and that you can't kill people who are already dead, let alone kill them with fact checking. As Kate Aronoff writes, a Gramscian war for cultural hegemony is being fought here, a war for the imagination, not for the truth.[3] It is self-explanatory that one of Trump's favoured 'news' outlets is called Infowars. 'Beware of the dreams of others, because if you get caught in their dream, you're screwed', as Gilles Deleuze said. It's up to us to make sure we have dreams bigger than theirs.[4]

As such, the galvanizing shock of collapsological studies has had a salutary effect. They open up a new imaginary, and although it's more of a nightmare than a dream, they have allowed many people to escape from the 'dreams of others'. But these studies are only really useful if they don't put us back to sleep immediately. How many of the young people who did not join the climate strike are already resigned because they have concluded from what they have read that there's nothing they can do to save themselves, that the ecological crisis is as unstoppable as some kind of natural disaster, or that, in any case, it is too big to be managed by even a large group of determined people? It is not, and part of making us believe it is part of the plot to discourage us. 'Ecology in one country', to paraphrase Stalin, could work, even more so across a continent: by drying up the revenues of even one major oil company, or a big chemical company, at the scale of states like France, Germany and Britain combined, a cascading bankruptcy effect could occur that would take down carbofascist strongholds.[5]

The battle against this rotting of minds that plays into the hands of carbofascism is an essential component of ecological and socialist struggle. 'Pessimists and skeptics must be driven out of the proletarian ranks, as carriers of a deadly infection', says Trotsky in the conclusion to one of his 1930s texts on the German situation. In fact, what can be done by political will can be undone by political will. 'They lie who say that the situation seems hopeless [. . .] The inner forces of the [. . .] proletariat are inexhaustible. They will clear the road for themselves.'⁶

Forces are shifting. Trumpism has been defeated – albeit temporarily. In Germany, the Greens – the only really structured environmental party in the world – are in a position to take power at the end of Angela Merkel's twilight reign and to bring the whole of Europe round in favour of the climate struggle. In Austria and France, the desire for ecological issues to be addressed is a rising threat to the neoliberal parties in power. The latter sense as much, and are worried about it. The crazy escalation of insults to Greta Thunberg testifies to this. There's panic afoot. Sick of waiting for grown-ups to act, children are taking to the streets all over the world every Friday by the millions. Civil society is waking up. Even Russian civil society is shifting, and Putin himself seems to be changing his mind about the benefits of global warming now that the melting permafrost is endangering gas drilling in Siberia.⁷ China is moving too, maybe triggered by massive floods and the risk of losing everything to the collapse of the Three Gorges Dam. Whereas Xi Jinping seemed to be determined to play the pyromaniac carbofascist firefighters at their own game by building two coal-fired power plants in the country for every one that is decommissioned in the West and securing supply lines in all directions, with the Silk Road in Asia and its neo-colonial expansion into Africa and South America, as if he were readying himself for a new Stalingrad, he has now pledged carbon neutrality by 2050. All over the world, the real political confrontation of our times is clarifying and crystallizing: it is not a conflict between the soft liberal centre and conservative sovereignism, but between ecosocialism and carbofascism.[8]

From the perspective of this confrontation, which clarifies the situation by forcing everyone to choose sides, environmentalists have to remember that communism would never have won its own fight against fascism, and would never have seduced so many people for so long, if it hadn't promised the proletariat 'tomorrows full of song'. It wouldn't have been enough for communism to have claimed that it wanted to save the world; it had to promise full employment, progress and even abundance. As Georges

Bataille once wrote of socialism, ecology should get used to saying that it

> does not just require the power of the people, but wealth as well. And no reasonable person can imagine it based on a world in which shanty towns would take the place of the civilization symbolized by the names of New York and London. That civilization is perhaps detestable; it sometimes seems to be only a bad dream; and there is no question that it generates the boredom and irritation that favour a slide toward catastrophe. But no one can reasonably consider something that only has the attraction of unreason in its favor.[9]

The bottom line is that the Anthropocene – as we now call the period during which human activity has influenced the earth's climate – is not only a nasty stain on humanity's impeccable curriculum vitae. It marks a bifurcation in the hominization process. The new capacity that we have acquired to affect the earth confronts us with its destiny and, in a certain sense, with its truth. The question before us is simple: do we want to live in the same way that our ancestors lived in the past upon this earth, subject to the hazards of the weather, viruses, famine, fire and flood, or do we want to assume and exercise the Promethean and ultimately infinitely poetic power to transform nature that is bestowed upon us by the powers of the mind? To say this does not imply any hubris. Neither it is simply 'solutionism'. By perpetuating this power to subject nature to its will, humanity is only exercising a gift it has received, and, precisely, received from nature after billions of years of evolution. Nature designed the mind, and designed it to extend itself. It doesn't ask for the respect or veneration that we owe only to the dead. Nature is alive, it wants to survive, and if it has to be disassembled in order to survive, if it must scale a thousand Golgothas, it is ready to do so. In fact, we could say that *not* helping nature to survive would amount to hubris: it would amount to believing that we are entitled to withdraw from the world's affairs and wash our hands of everything that lives under the sun, in the name of a principle foreign and superior to nature – *that* would be megalomaniac.

We are no longer the Easter Islanders described by Jared Diamond, a people who died out because of their own activity of deforestation. We have grown to the stature of the moai, the basalt giants they built along their coasts to protect them. We have the potential, or rather the duty, to take control of the thermodynamic cycle of the planet as we once took control of the reproductive cycle of life – and think of the effort it took to achieve that, and how the right to control one's body is still contested today by all the anti-abortion activists in the world! We cannot be for that right and against this duty.

Gaia must not be deprived of *her* hopes.

The World is Ours!

In the 1930s, Bataille met a physicist who taught him the basics of thermodynamics. Bataille wrote a book entitled *The Accursed Share*, the working title of which, however, was for a long time *Economics on the Scale of the Universe*. He was attempting to conceive of a human economy that would imitate nature, a kind of cosmic communism capable of overcoming the double impasse of capitalism and sovietism. A project that is still germane today. Indeed, perhaps it is the great political project that our times have long been calling for.

In many ways it was already the project of Marx, who was the fascinated contemporary of the works of Sadi Carnot, Rudolf Clausius,

Hermann von Helmholtz and James Prescott Joule which led to the discovery of the concept of energy and the popularization of the idea that the entire universe, and perhaps even life, respond to two principles of startling simplicity: the principle of energy conservation (nothing is lost, everything is transformed) and the principle of energy dissipation (nothing is lost, but everything is diluted). The reason why Marxism remains relevant against all odds is that Marx thought it was possible to extend the laws of physics discovered by thermodynamics to society and the economy, by identifying the concept of energy with that of labour. Before Marx, economists' scientific models were borrowed from the physics of so-called 'equilibrium' dynamic systems such as the orbits of the planets, governed by the deterministic laws of action and reaction. These models, which assume that societies achieve optima under perfect conditions of exchange between supply and demand, form the basis of the so-called neoclassical school of economics. But they give us a totally abstract and false vision of nature and, consequently, they lead to the creation of a totally abstract and false vision of society. They justify inequalities in the name of a truncated science. Against them, Marx thought that social justice would be restored by establishing the scientific truth of nature and society. His idea of communism was to replace the founding mechanistic action–reaction model of capitalism with the thermodynamic action–retroaction model.

Of course, he failed to bring this about, even within his own political movement. Despite what science has taught us about dynamic far-from-equilibrium systems, we continue to use linear models of growth, models that simply don't work. To pests we opposed short-term remedies – pesticides, which called for a whole cascade of other equally short-term remedies, pesticide-resistant genetically modified seeds, seeds that finally did their job so well that today there is nothing left in places, neither pests nor the birds that once fed on them; and soon there will be no plants left either – rather than taking into account the totality of the cycle of life in a dynamic manner. Similarly, we opposed short-term solutions to recent economic crises – programmes of austerity, tax cuts, massive injections of liquidity into banks – measures that have only helped further widen inequalities and made the crises to come even more dangerous, rather than massively investing in research, education, healthcare and infrastructure.

But it is up to us to reinitiate the Marxist project. And it is ultimately in the name of the concrete struggle against carbofascism that we can (re)discover this new paradigm, rather than some abstract struggle against capitalism. The mobilization that forces us to temporarily set aside the project of breaking with capitalism is the very thing that makes it possible to make this break real. By forcing us to invent a tax on negative externalities, by forcing us to learn to control the carbon cycle, by teaching us once again how to coproduce our society along with nature, by replacing the concept of growth with that of energy efficiency[1] and, in general, by reconciling ourselves with our place and role in the universe, the breaking point towards which carbofascism compels us is also the tipping point that makes the revolution possible. To paraphrase French environmentalist philosopher Pierre Charbonnier, in rallying to the ecological cause, we perceive 'that it is not just one democratic issue among others', but that democracy itself proceeds 'from the ecological exigency'.[2]

There are still many other things to do and say

in order to triumph, of course. Since the 1930s, thinking on the 'bio-economy' has continued to proliferate and deepen, from the work of chemist Frederick Soddy[3] on a financial system compatible with the principles of thermodynamics, to those of economists Bernard Lietaer[4] and François Roddier[5] on monetary polyculture, as well as the foundational work of Nicholas Georgescu-Roegen[6] and especially René Passet,[7] both of whom refer to the need for new development indicators and for a reopening of the question of a planned economy. This is not the place to review all of these works. For now, let it suffice to know that we not only have justice on our side, we also have reason and history. All we need now is the will. Or rather, the fortitude. For, in the end, fighting global warming and the extinction of biodiversity is more a question of dignity than of survival. As has been said, carbofascism also offers 'solutions'. They are no less effective. But they are repulsive solutions that appeal to our basest sentiments. As long as we are lucky enough to live in the West, to be white and to have a bit of money saved, they sing in our ears, like sirens, that we will emerge victorious from the climate disaster without having to do anything, just live and let die, omitting to mention that the winners we will be, when we come out of this affair, will have ceased to be human beings altogether.

Fiat justitia, et pereat mundus, as a Roman saying has it: 'Let justice be done, though the world perish.' We must see to it that justice is done *so that* the world may be saved. We must take back the world as the sans-culottes took the Bastille, as the insurgents of 1917 took the Summer Palace, because this world is ours, it belongs to us, and it is because it has been stolen from us that justice is no longer done. Then we can build a society that is 'the true resolution of the strife between man and nature' and achieve 'the true resurrection of nature – the naturalism of man and the humanism of nature both brought to fulfilment'.[8]

Notes

1 A New Front

1 https://www.theguardian.com/australia-news/2017/oct/10/tony-abbott-says-climate-change-is-probably-doing-good.

2 'A massive 200 billion dollar sea wall, built around New York to protect it from rare storms, is a costly, foolish & environmentally unfriendly idea that, when needed, probably won't work anyway. It will also look terrible. Sorry, you'll just have to get your mops & buckets ready!', @realdonaldtrump, 19 January 2020.

2 Short the World

1 Address given 23 September 2019, https://www.fridaysforfuture.org.

2 N. Klein, *The Shock Doctrine* (Toronto: Random House Canada, 2007).

3 Some of them can be heard admitting this quite openly in Jérôme Fritel's documentary *Main Basse sur l'eau* (Arte, 2018).

3 Reichstag Megafires

1 N. Klein, *On Fire : The Burning Case for a Green New Deal* (London: Allen Lane, 2019).

2 See 'Ecofascisme: comment l'extrême-droite en ligne s'est réappropriée les questions climatiques', *Le Monde*, 4 October 2019.

3 It is no coincidence that Jean Raspail's obscure 1970s bestseller, *Le Camp des Saints*, which tells the story of how a flood of migrants is overwhelming Europe, is once again on the nightstands of the European far right (Samuel Huntington, the author of *The Clash of Civilizations*, has a lot of praise for it). On climate wars see also M. Butler, *Climate Wars* (Melbourne: Melbourne University Press, 2017), and the very dark warnings at the conclusion of Kate Aronoff's *A Planet to Win: Why We Need a Green New Deal* (London: Verso, 2019).

4 The concept of the deconstruction of the state was formulated by Bannon at the February 2017 Conservative Political Action Conference at National Harbor, Maryland. The empty-chair policy practised by the Trump cabinet since then, which has left gaping holes in the administration, is probably a deliberate implementation of this strategy, rather than a sign of Trump's autocratic tendencies or incompetence.

5 The remarks were made at a press conference at the Arctic Forum in Arkhangelsk, 30 March 2017.
6 George Monbiot has shown the connection between the two types of disaster capitalism ruling Brexit and 'Earthxit': https://www.theguardian.com/comment isfree/2020/nov/24/brexit-capitalism.
7 A. Rees-Mogg, 'How to Profit from the World's Water Crisis', *MoneyWeek*, 5 November 2017.
8 Some conspiracists are genuinely convinced that vegans want to feminize men by forcing them to ingest 'phytoestrogens' that are found in large quantities in vegetables, especially soya, because they conflate them with 'oestrogens', a female hormonal marker that has nothing to do with phytoestrogens.

4 'So They Knew . . .'

1 The first official report on climate change commissioned by the American Senate, the 'Charney Report', dates from 1979.
2 Stanton A. Glantz, John Slade, Lisa A. Bero, Peter Hanauer and Deborah E. Barnes, *The Cigarette Papers* (Berkeley: University of California Press, 1998).
3 As shown by G. Chamayou, *La société ingouvernable: une généalogie du libéralisme autoritaire* (Paris: La Fabrique, 2018), 125; translated by Andrew Brown as *The Ungovernable Society* (Cambridge: Polity, forthcoming).
4 The establishment of 'armed civic guards' to deal

with these state militias, as recommended by Murray Bookchin, for example, just seems like a bad joke in such a scenario.

5 Cf. M. B. Petersen, M. Osmundsen and K. Arceneaux, 'A "Need for Chaos" and the Sharing of Hostile Political Rumors in Advanced Democracies', *PsyArXiv*, 1 September 2018.

6 Darwin believed that human societies owe their superiority over animal societies precisely to the fact that the former care for the weakest, so that they develop an empathy that strengthens bonds and enables them to develop more complex societies. He was therefore opposed to the application of natural selection to society *precisely for evolutionary reasons*.

5 Carbofascism

1 B. Latour, *Down to Earth: Politics in the New Climatic Regime* (Cambridge: Polity, 2018).

2 https://www.ohchr.org/Documents/Issues/Pover ty/A_HRC_41_39.pdf.

3 Including fossil fuels, which explains the tensions mounting around Iran and Saudi Arabia, the paradox of the situation being that only more energy can help combat the damage caused by too much energy.

4 See E. Mandel, 'Leon Trotsky's Theory of Fascism', *New Left Review*, 1:47, January–February 1968.

5 J.-B. Fressoz, 'Bolsonaro, Trump, Duterte: la montée d'un-carbo-fascisme?', *Libération*, 10 October 2018.

6 George Monbiot says: 'The US was lucky to get Trump – Biden may pave the way for a more competent autocrat', https://www.theguardian.com/commentisfree/2020/nov/11/us-trump-biden-president-elect.

6 ACT UP for the Climate

1 See D. Tanuro, 'Le lourd héritage écologique de Léon Trotski', published on the website of the Nouveau Parti Anticapitaliste, https://www.anti-k.org/2018/09/05/ecologie-le-lourd-heritage-de-leon-trotsky-par-daniel-tanuro.

2 L. Kramer, *Reports from the Holocaust: The Making of an AIDS Activist* (New York: St. Martin's Press, 1989 [1994]). On how environmentalists can be inspired by ACT UP: M. K. Salamon, *Facing the Climate Emergency: How to Transform Yourself with Climate Truth* (Gabriola: New Society, 2020).

7 This is Not a Crisis

1 This is one of the Club of Rome's three essential recommendations, along with the development of family planning in developing countries and support for research in developed countries.

2 J. Boyce, *The Case for Carbon Dividends* (Cambridge: Polity, 2019).

8 The Green Army

1 L. Phillips, *Austerity Ecology & the Collapse-Porn*

Addicts: A Defence of Growth, Progress, Industry and Stuff (London: Zero Books, 2015).

2 P. Newell and A. Simms go so far as to say we need a 'non-proliferation treaty' ('Towards a Fossil Fuel Non-Proliferation Treaty', *Climate Policy*, 20:8, 2019.)

3 Non-profits are already working on this across the world, although to give some idea of the enormity of the task, purchasing only 10 per cent of French arable land would cost 10 billion euros (200 euros per French citizen).

4 On this point, we salute the courage of Holly Jean Buck, who takes these questions head on from an ecological point of view in *After Geoengineering: Climate Tragedy, Repair and Restoration* (London: Verso, 2019).

5 Remember that James Lovelock ruled out neither nuclear power nor geo-engineering, and the same goes for the experts of the IPCC, all of whose scenarios count upon the latter.

6 Over the last ten years, the American government committed $5 billion dollars to carbon capture and storage (CCS). Notwithstanding the fact that CCS is a particular and debatable mode of carbon control (one that relies on being plugged into polluting factories), such an amount of money is ridiculously small. As a comparison, the New York Police Department's operating budget alone is twice that amount *per year* ($10.9 billion in 2020).

7 The phrase is Sarah Schulman's: see 'What ACT UP Can Teach Us About the Current Health Emergency', *Frieze Magazine*, June 2020.

8 Greenhouse gas inventories have been mandated since the 1997 Kyoto Protocol.

9 https://www.theguardian.com/environment/2019/mar/22/dirty-lies-how-the-car-industry-hid-the-truth-about-diesel-emissions.

10 On the subject of Green realpolitik, see also A. Lievin, *Climate Change and the Nation State* (Harmondsworth: Penguin, 2020).

9 Gaia Must Not Be Deprived of Her Hopes

1 P.-H. Castel, *Le Mal qui vient* (Paris: Cerf, 2018).

2 The authors of a survey on populism clearly showed that the dividing line between a vote for right-wing populism and a vote for left-wing populism was the degree of trust we have in humanity in general, and in particular in our friends and relatives. See D. Cohen, M. Foucault and Y. Algan, *The Origins of Populism* (New York: Threshold, 2019).

3 Aronoff, *A Planet to Win*.

4 G. Deleuze, 'Qu'est-ce que l'acte de création?', *Fémis*, 17 May 1987.

5 David Holmgren calls for a democratically engineered financial crash to that effect; see *Future Scenarios: How Communities Can Adapt to Peak Oil and Climate Change: Mapping the Cultural*

Implications of Peak Oil and Climate Change (White River Junction, VT: Green Books, 2009).

6 L. Trotsky, 'What Next? Vital Questions for the German Proletariat' (1932), https://www.marxists. org/archive/trotsky/germany/1932-ger.

7 'Why Vladimir Putin Suddenly Believes in Global Warming', *Bloomberg*, 29 September 2019.

8 In 1991 the 13th Congress of the Fourth International expressed its commitment to socialism becoming an ecosocialism. Unfortunately, what it meant by this was just a harmless variant of frugalism, which not only has no chance of seeing the light of day, but is also incompatible with Marxism itself – see above.

9 G. Bataille, *The Accursed Share, Vol. 1: Consumption*, translated by Robert Hurley (New York: Zone, 1988), 170.

10 The World is Ours!

1 As the astrophysicist François Roddier recalls, the law that governs thermodynamics, and by extension the evolution of living beings, is not growth, but efficiency in the operation of dissipation and entropy ('maximum entropy production'). See F. Roddier, *Thermodynamique de l'évolution* (Paris: Editions Parole, 2012).

2 P. Charbonnier, 'L'écologie, c'est réinventer le progrès social', interview with the journal *Ballast*, 2018, https://www.revue-ballast.fr/pierre-charbonnier-lec ologie-cest-reinventer-lidee-de-progres-social. See

also V. Chansigaud, *Les Français et la nature* (Arles: Actes Sud, 2017).

3 F. Soddy, *Money Versus Man: A Statement of the World Problem from the Standpoint of the New Economics* (New York: E. P. Dutton, 1933).

4 B. Lietaer, *Halte à la toute-puissance des banques* (Paris: Odile Jacob, 2012).

5 F. Roddier, *De la thermodynamique à l'économie: Le tourbillon de la vie* (Paris: Editions Paroles, 2018).

6 N. Georgescu-Roegen, *Pour une révolution bio-économique* (Lyon: ENS Editions, 2013).

7 R. Passet, *L'économique et le vivant* (Paris: Economica, 1979, new edn 1996).

8 K. Marx, *Economic and Philosophic Manuscripts of 1844*, translated and edited by Martin Milligan (Mineola, NY: Dover, 2007), 102, 104.